W9-CAZ-044

The Funniest Man in Baseball

THE TRUE STORY OF MAX PATKIN

Audrey Vernick

Illustrated by Jennifer Bower

CLARION BOOKS | Houghton Mifflin Harcourt | Boston   New York

CLARION BOOKS

3 Park Avenue, New York, New York 10016

Text copyright © 2018 by Audrey Vernick
Illustrations copyright © 2018 by Jennifer Bower

Clarion Books is an imprint of
Houghton Mifflin Harcourt Publishing Company.

hmhco.com

The illustrations were rendered in pencil and Adobe Photoshop
with Kyle Webster's Gouache & Dry Media brushes.
The text was set in Proxima Nova.
Book design by Sharismar Rodriguez

Library of Congress Cataloging-in-Publication Data is available.
ISBN 978-0-544-81377-9

Manufactured in China
SCP 10 9 8 7 6 5 4 3 2 1
4500692217

For human baseball encyclopedia Tim Wiles, with thanks for all the inspiration —A.V.

To my amazing daughter, who reminds me daily to pursue my dreams with humor and gusto! —J.B.

HOT ROASTED Peanuts

DID YOU HEAR the one about the pitcher who walked into a ballpark? He turned into a clown!

No, seriously!

TRUE STORY!

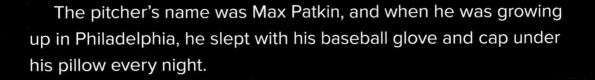

The pitcher's name was Max Patkin, and when he was growing up in Philadelphia, he slept with his baseball glove and cap under his pillow every night.

He worked to become a high-kicking fastball pitcher, playing in sandlot games and then straight through high school and into the minor leagues.

He was a funny guy, a goofy guy, always looking for a laugh,

but serious about becoming a major-league pitcher.

Max hurt his elbow in a game in 1942. Too injured to keep playing ball, he joined the navy. World War II was raging and many Americans were signing up to serve their country.

PROPERTY OF U.S. NAVY 42099

While he was at boot camp in Illinois, a surgeon operated on his elbow.

After three months of recovery, Max discovered he could still pitch well.

Greetings FROM **HAII**

He was shipped to Honolulu, Hawaii, where, it turned out, the armed forces were looking for professional ballplayers to entertain the troops.

Lucky Max.

Many major-league baseball players had enlisted. One of Max's teammates was the great Brooklyn Dodger Pee Wee Reese. His opponents were a pretty big deal too.

On one fateful day, the team Max pitched against had a player named Joe DiMaggio on the roster.

The same Joe DiMaggio who'd already hit more than 200 home runs as a New York Yankee—a true superstar!

The first time Max faced DiMaggio,
Max struck him out!

But on his next at-bat, DiMaggio hit the ball so hard, some people think it's still flying somewhere in the sky.

Max could never explain what made him do what he did next, but he threw his glove and left the mound to follow Joltin' Joe all the way around the bases, pumping his arms, making faces, and mimicking the way DiMaggio ran.

When Max reached home plate, everyone from both teams was there to shake his hand, congratulate him, to tell him how funny he was. Usually the guy who hits the home run is greeted with high-fives and cheers, but "there's DiMaggio sitting by himself in an empty dugout," as Max later recalled.

TRUE STORY!

People loved it! The commanding officer kept receiving calls asking when the goofy guy would be pitching again. "I was like a hero," Max said.

After the war, determined to pursue his dream, Max signed to play with a Cleveland Indians farm team. On the sidelines, he was still a goofball. But he knew his performance on the mound really mattered.

He was pitching in the minor leagues again, hoping to work his way up to the majors.

But after *another* injury—his shoulder this time—Max was released by the team.

Disappointed that his major-league dreams had slipped away, he returned home to Philadelphia. It was then that Max received a call asking him to do his comic routine at an exhibition game. In those days, there were no mascots walking around stadiums in costume. There had been some "baseball clowns"—funny men performing baseball-related acts before the game to warm up the crowd. Al Schacht was the most famous of them.

CLEVELA

But Max's performance was different in a very big way—he did his act *during* the game.

In a game between the Cleveland Indians and its Harrisburg farm team, Max showed up and did his bit. He stood in the first-base coaching box, using typical signs like tapping his arm and touching his cap, but before long, he was swinging his hips, dancing on the foul line, and flapping his arms like a bird.

The crowd went wild!

Word reached the Indians' owner, Bill Veeck. Before long, Max signed on to perform and clown-coach at Cleveland Indians games—the big leagues!

Max's very first day was one he and 80,000 fans never forgot. It happened to be a day when three Hall of Famers—Ty Cobb, Babe Ruth, and Tris Speaker—were being honored, and it was standing room only at Cleveland Municipal Stadium. Fans were roaring even before the game began.

Max worried the crowd
might not find him funny,
but he went out there, stood in the
first-base coaching box, and ran
through his act, growing more
and more ridiculous.

He imitated the way players ran.

He danced and showed off his
moves and was an all-around
baseball clown.

"They laughed hard,"
Max said later.

On the field, Max, a tall, skinny guy, was never hard to spot.

He used to say,
"I looked like a nose on the end of
a lollipop stick." His uniform was very baggy—
better suited to a scarecrow than a ballplayer.
Instead of PATKIN on the back, there was a big
question mark. His body was so loose and
fluid that it almost seemed as though
it were made out of a different kind
of bones—rubbery ones,
maybe.

Then there was his face. Bill Veeck said Max looked like he'd been put
together by someone who couldn't read the instructions very well.

Max would do anything to get a laugh.

"It's in my blood," he said. "It's a great feeling to know that I can make people laugh. Especially families, kids. They're my best audience."

Max began booking appearances at minor-league ballparks—
and that's where he worked for decades.

As Max's reputation grew, so did his routine. He'd be on the field during
the third, fourth, and fifth innings, spitting water on players, kissing base
runners, playing hopscotch.

Fans loved his bat trick, in which he'd sling two armfuls of baseball bats over his shoulder, then take a comic fall, the bats rolling in all directions.

He used to "lose" his pants and run around in an old-time bathing suit.

With "Rock Around the Clock" blasting, he'd perform a crazy coach-giving-ridiculous-signs dance.

The crowd favorite was usually "the fountain." Max would take a huge gulp of soda and spew geysers straight up—way, way up—from his mouth. He averaged fifteen to twenty spurts per gulp. His record was forty.

At the end of his act, Max would crawl between the catcher's legs, offer a batting lesson (holding the wrong end of the bat), and then hit a ball and race to third base,

where he'd kick up dust and get into a comic fight with the umpire, who would throw him out of the game.

Before long, Max Patkin was famous
throughout the minor leagues. Once Al Schacht
retired, Max was the only baseball clown out
there. And he would be the last, because
teams started turning to mascots for
entertainment. Max did not approve.
He was very proud of the work
he did. "They're laughing at me,
my face, my body when they
laugh. You know what they
laugh at now? Men in costumes.
That's how baseball's sideshow
entertainment has evolved, from
clowns to chickens." But those
mascots were no real competition
for Max—he kept working for years
as baseball's only clown.

One of Max's favorite stories to tell was about a summer afternoon in July 1969. Crowds always came out for Max. But that day in Grand Falls, Montana, Max performed for a total of four people. Four!

No one was thinking of baseball. More than half a billion people were home watching astronauts Neil Armstrong and Buzz Aldrin take the first-ever walk on the moon, even though the manager had offered to set up televisions in the ballpark.

Two of the four people in attendance, Max liked to say, were the starting pitcher's parents.

TRUE STORY!

Max's comedy was very physical and led to a lot of injuries—broken ribs, toes, and fingers, a bad back. None of that kept him from showing up at every appearance he booked. It wasn't always easy. He once had to fly in the back of a mail plane, surrounded by letters and packages.

He raced after buses,

took a taxi with a flat tire for hundreds of miles,
bummed rides—whatever it took.

He traveled vast distances from ballpark to ballpark,
meeting players who would remember Max forever.

"When I look at the list of Hall of Famers
and realize I've worked with so many of them,
it makes my head spin."

Max used to say, only half joking, that his streak for consecutive appearances was more impressive than Cal Ripken's famous record of playing in 2,632 games in a row. Max Patkin showed up for more than 4,000 before retiring at age seventy-five.

His streak ended—of all things!—on a day he wasn't even scheduled to work. Max tripped on the clubhouse steps at Fenway Park. He sprained his ankle and missed his next scheduled appearance.

But it had been a great run. Through it all, Max had a front-row seat—an on-the-field seat!—to nearly five decades of baseball. He crawled between the legs of Yogi Berra.

He saw Babe Ruth
take his last swing.

He goofed around with Hank Greenberg and
Harmon Killebrew at first base.

"Nobody has had more fun than I have," Max said. "In my heart I would have rather been a big-league baseball player. But then I'd have never made so many people happy."

So did you hear the one about the kid from Philadelphia whose childhood dream took a funny turn? In the end, it was a kind of amazing, hilarious, surprising, wild ride.

Author's Note

FOR YOUNG MAX PATKIN, it all started with a trip to Philadelphia's Shibe Park, where he fell in love with baseball. From that day on, Max got to work in the game that he loved, practicing hard for a career on the field—as a pitcher in the major leagues.

He got half his wish. Max spent more years on the baseball diamond than any professional player ever could, but instead of focusing on strikeouts, Max was always striving for the maximum number of laughs per minute.

What he never could have imagined was that he would become a lifelong memory for thousands of

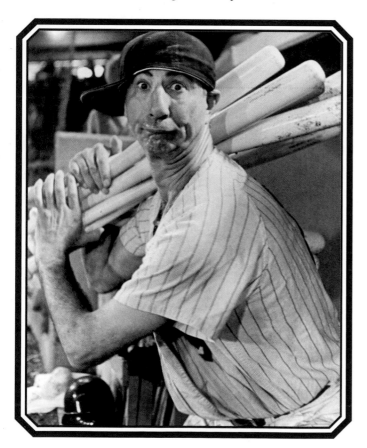

ballplayers. When former minor-leaguer Ron Shelton decided he wanted to write a screenplay about his years in baseball (*Bull Durham,* a movie for adults), he knew he had to include Max Patkin. Every minor-league ballplayer had seen Max do his routine. Many times. It was an essential part of life in the minor leagues.

"Reggie Jackson always remembered seeing me in Lewiston," Max said proudly. "Mickey Mantle knew it was somewhere in Oklahoma."

Even though Max Patkin did not end up with the life he had envisioned, his career was a magical one, spanning five decades. He loved talking about his long afternoons and evenings at ballparks all over the country, the players he met, the publicity stunts he'd witnessed, the amazing firsts and lasts and never-agains. Some of the stories sounded unbelievable, even to Max, and he was there when they happened! That's why he'd often add "true story" at the end. It was Max's version of "happily ever after."

BIBLIOGRAPHY

"Clown Hall of Fame to Induct Six." *Racine Journal Times,* January 17, 1991.

Goldstein, Richard. "Max Patkin, 79, Clown Prince of Baseball." *New York Times,* November 1, 1999.

"Max Patkin on Bull Durham." Interview by John C. Tibbetts. YouTube, February 8, 2011. Accessed June 1, 2015.

"Max Patkin TV Interview 1990." YouTube, September 9, 2013. Accessed June 2, 2015.

Minor League Baseball. "King of Baseball Award." MILB.com Major Award Winners, 2016. August 10, 2016. www.milb.com/milb/history/awards. jsp?#king; accessed June 28, 2017.

Patkin, Max, and Stan Hochman. *The Clown Prince of Baseball.* Waco, Tex.: WRS Pub., 1994.

Sports Reference LLC. "Joe DiMaggio." Baseball-Reference.com—Major League Statistics and Information. www.baseball-reference.com; accessed June 12, 2015.

Tibbetts, John C. "Max Patkin on Bull Durham." YouTube, February 8, 2011. Accessed June 2, 2015.

Wulf, Steve. "Max: After More Than 40 Years, The Clown Prince of Baseball, Max Patkin, Still Leaves 'Em Laughing." *Sports Illustrated,* June 6, 1988. Sports Illustrated Vault: www.si.com/vault; accessed June 28, 2017.